MW00978789

This book belongs to

# fill me in
## * with friends

**Illustrations by Jo Harrison**

**Edited by Kaitlin Olson**

TOUCHSTONE

New York   London   Toronto   Sydney   New Delhi

Touchstone
An Imprint of Simon & Schuster, Inc.
1230 Avenue of the Americas
New York, NY 10020

First Touchstone hardcover edition November 2018

TOUCHSTONE and colophon are registered trademarks of Simon & Schuster, Inc.

For information about special discounts for bulk purchases,
please contact Simon & Schuster Special Sales at 1-866-506-1949
or business@simonandschuster.com.

The Simon & Schuster Speakers Bureau can bring authors to your live event.
For more information or to book an event, contact the Simon & Schuster Speakers Bureau
at 866-248-3049 or visit our website at www.simonspeakers.com.

Design by Phil M. Ian

Manufactured in the United States of America

1  3  5  7  9  10  8  6  4  2

ISBN 978-1-5011-9479-5

fill me in

# How to Use This Book

Hello, friends!

If you're anything like me, you'll skip right over this page, which is probably why board game rules change every time I play. For someone quite good at following directions, I certainly love to ignore them.

This book is inspired by my friends: by late night discussions, by conversation starter packs, by contested games of Cards Against Humanity, by predictions of what our lives will look like in ten, twenty, and fifty years.

Inside, you'll find three sections: Past, Superlatives, and Future. The Past section holds memories from the beginning of your friendship to the present. The Future section allows you to make predictions for both your lives and your friendship. And Superlatives are like your high school yearbook superlatives—if only they were more fun (I was voted "most likely to win a Grammy Award" in high school, but here I am writing books!).

You can complete this book with one best friend or with a larger group. Many questions ask you to write in or circle your answer. I suggest that if your friend(s) agrees with your answer, he/she/they can initial next to it. If more than one friend wants to circle the same answer, use your initials. I recommend using different colored pens, but it's by no means required. You can use one journal as a group keepsake or give every friend a journal.

I hope that this journal will spark conversation (and some extremely creative *Real Housewives* taglines), bring back good memories, and help you get to know your friends just a little bit better. To spread the love, please feel free to share at #fillmeinjournal. There are few things that bring more joy than friendship. And I'm sure all your friends are great, but mine are the best.

— Kaitlin Olson

*Fill Me In* editor,
friendship evangelist,
and most likely to dump someone
for being "too nice"

past

Let's start with an easy exercise:
## write your names
(and initials, which will be useful later on).

**NAME:**                    **INITIALS:**

## Write the story of your friendship.

## How and when did you meet?

**What was your first impression
of one another?**

**How did your impression change
once you got to know one another?**

## What are three adjectives your friends would use to describe you?

Write them here or initial around the figure at right.

What is your biggest flaw?
Be honest.

What is the nicest thing a friend
has done for you?

**What qualities do you value most in a friendship?**

**CIRCLE OR INITIAL ALL THAT APPLY.**

keeps secrets well          always answers texts

good taste in music          up for an adventure

prefers staying in          funny

encouraging          will laugh at any joke

**OTHER:**

## What is your strongest group value?

**CIRCLE OR INITIAL ONE.**

willing to try anything          honesty          loyalty

hates everyone else          alcohol consumption

best to party with          good gossip

won't make new friends

**OTHER:**

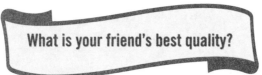

What is your friend's best quality?

If playing in a group, write the best quality of the person on your left. Pass the journal around and initial if you agree with the assessment, or add your own.

## Who is your friend's worst ex?

## Who is your biggest cheerleader?

If you were to cheer up a friend,
how would you do it?

What's the word/saying/catchphrase
your friend uses all the time?

**CIRCLE OR INITIAL YOUR ANSWER.**

totally          YAASS          it me

obsessed          OMG stahp          bb

basic AF          yeah, duh          I cannot

literally          bae          The struggle is real

I'm dead          actually

**OTHER:**

(E) Extraversion/Introversion (I)

(S) Sensing/Intuition (N)

(T) Thinking/Feeling (F)

(J) Judging/Perceiving (P)

| | | | |
|---|---|---|---|
| **ISTJ** | **ISFJ** | **INFJ** | **INTP** |
| **ISTP** | **ISFP** | **INFP** | **INTP** |
| **ESTP** | **ESFP** | **ENFP** | **ENTP** |
| **ESTJ** | **ESFJ** | **ENFJ** | **ENTJ** |

What was your first form of social media?
Write your username/handle here.

| Email | AIM | Instagram | Snapchat |
|---|---|---|---|
| _____ | _____ | _____ | _____ |
| _____ | _____ | _____ | _____ |
| _____ | _____ | _____ | _____ |
| _____ | _____ | _____ | _____ |
| _____ | _____ | _____ | _____ |
| _____ | _____ | _____ | _____ |
| _____ | _____ | _____ | _____ |
| _____ | _____ | _____ | _____ |

**OTHER: LiveJournal, Xanga, Myspace, Neopets**

Pick a hashtag that best encapsulates
each of your friends and/or group.

**CIRCLE OR INITIAL YOUR ANSWERS.**

#goobs          #squadgoals          #beyhive

#coachellaweek3          #fitspo          #gurlgroup4evah

#instagood          #avotoast          #extremelylatergram

#millennialpink          #coffeecoffeecoffee          #friendzone

#resist          #doesn'tknowhowtousehashtags

#nerdfamily          #potterhead

#sorrynotsorry

**OTHER:**

If you were to write a Facebook
or Instagram birthday appreciation post
right now, what would it say?

Guess the top five emojis
on your friend's phone.
Draw them here.

**NAME:**

**EMOJIS:**

# What is your friend's best selfie?

## Please describe or draw it
in as detailed a manner as possible.

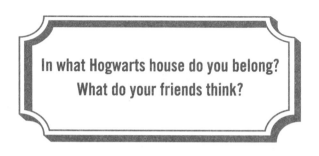

In what Hogwarts house do you belong?
What do your friends think?

**CIRCLE YOUR ANSWERS.**

If you agree with your friend's choice, please initial beside it.

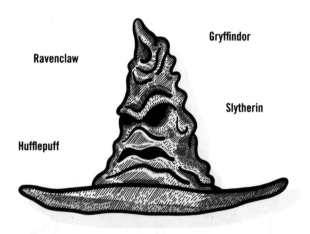

Ravenclaw

Gryffindor

Slytherin

Hufflepuff

## What's your theme song?

**What is one (or several) TV show(s) you all love?**

Mash the plots of your favorite TV shows
to create a new one.

**FOR EXAMPLE:**

*Vanderpump Rules* + *Mindhunter*:
Stassi's fascination with all things murder
becomes too real, and she starts investigating
cold cases with the help of her loyal podcast listeners.

Cast your friends as the characters in *Friends*.
Careful who you pick as your Ross.

*(Come on, no one wants to be Ross.)*

**THE FRIENDS:**

Rachel

Monica

Phoebe

Joey

Ross

Chandler

**THE ACQUAINTANCES:**

**CIRCLE OR INITIAL YOUR ANSWERS.**

Janice          Emily          Richard

Ugly Naked Guy          Emma          Jack Geller

Nora Bing          Phoebe's Grandma          Carol

**EXPLAIN YOUR CHOICES:**

# What is your Cheers/JJ's Diner/Rick's Cafe/Luke's Diner?

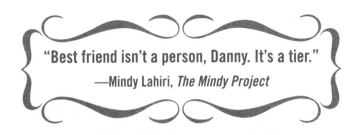

"Best friend isn't a person, Danny. It's a tier."
—Mindy Lahiri, *The Mindy Project*

**YOUR INITIALS:**                    **YOUR TIER:**

**What is the best book recommendation a friend gave you?**

Read this...

# Which Emma are you? Initial beside one.

Woodhouse

Stone

Watson

Thompson

## What literary hero(ine) are you?

**CIRCLE OR INITIAL YOUR ANSWER.**

Don Quixote               Elizabeth Bennet

Atticus Finch             Holly Golightly

Miss Havisham             Patrick Bateman

Hermione Granger          Sula Peace

Éowyn        Holden Caulfield        Matilda

Daenerys Targaryen

**OTHER:**

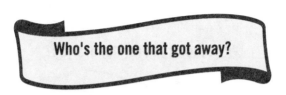

Who's the one that got away?

Who were your teenage celebrity crushes?

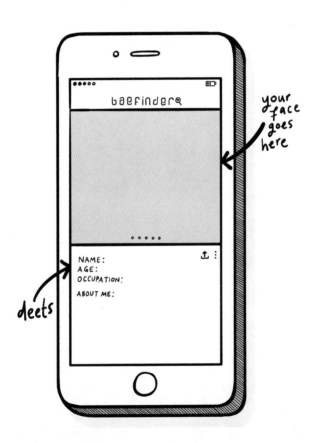

What would your dating profile say
if it were 100% honest?

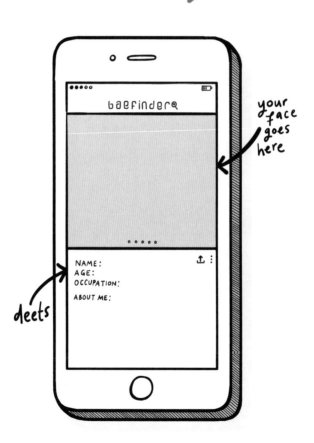

Write or splash your favorite drink here. What's your best story involving this drink?

Using people you all know (celebrities welcome), what's the hardest Marry/Fuck/Kill you can come up with?

**If you were an animal,
what would you be?**

Specifics (breed, color, origin)
are encouraged.

And now for a brief interlude. Please color
the page at right featuring cats eating takeout.

What is the most meaningful
material possession you own?

# What is the best gift you have received?

# Share the best gossip you've heard.

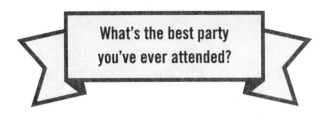

**What's the best party you've ever attended?**

Draw or otherwise describe your friends
and have them guess who is who.

**You will be judged on accuracy,
not artistic skill.**

Write the story your friend
won't stop telling.

What's your favorite topic of discussion with friends?

**What is the best advice you've ever received?**

**What deepest, darkest secrets have you shared with your friends?**

Feel free to write them *all* here.

What do you want to remember
about this time in your life?

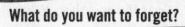

What do you want to forget?

**What was the best thing to happen to you in the last twelve months?**

# How have you changed over the last three to five years?

# superlatives

LOVE

## Most likely to . . .

(Draw a line between the options and your names.)

**NAMES:**

fall in love with a new person
every week

_____

dump someone for being "too
nice"

_____

run off with the pretender to a
foreign throne

_____

delete and re-download Tinder
fifty times

_____

elope in Vegas

_____

marry for money

_____

die alone

_____

sleep with a celebrity

_____

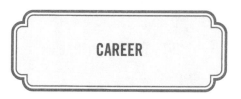

## CAREER

**Most likely to . . .**

(Draw a line between the options and your names.)

**NAMES:**

become CEO

_____

be a motivational speaker

_____

get arrested in an SEC
investigation

_____

quit the rat race and move
to Vermont

_____

change jobs every year

_____

make a 30 under 30 list
(or 40 under 40, etc.)

_____

star in a reality TV show

_____

start her own business

_____

**Most likely to . . .**

(Draw a line between the options and your names.)

**NAMES:**

cancel plans at the last minute     _____

pretend to be sick to get out of
a commitment     _____

bring a book to a party     _____

show up forty minutes late     _____

leave a party without saying
goodbye     _____

never talk to us again     _____

use "exciting night" to describe
reading a book in the tub     _____

ignore the group chat for months
at a time     _____

**DELINQUENTS**

## Most likely to . . .

(Draw a line between the options and your names.)

**NAMES:**

dance on a table                          _____

get kicked out of a public place          _____

need bail money                           _____

try to make it as a stand-up
comedian                                  _____

forget to file taxes                      _____

get a DUI                                 _____

bring a controlled substance
over an international border               _____

go on more than three dates
in one night                              _____

**MISCELLANY**

## Most likely to . . .

(Draw a line between the options and your names.)

**NAMES:**

glow up                                    _____

write a tell-all                           _____

win a Grammy Award                         _____

have a tweet go viral                      _____

start a club                               _____

receive a glowing obituary                 _____

win the lottery                            _____

start a rumor                              _____

**MORE MISCELLANY**

## Most likely to . . .

(Draw a line between the options and your names.)

**NAMES:**

make a burn book                                    _____

reference _____ (movie)                         _____

insult a significant other's
parents                                             _____

survive in Westeros                                 _____

start a lifestyle blog                              _____

be the first to make $1 million                     _____

crash a wedding                                     _____

die young                                           _____

*future*

How do you hope to change
in the next three to five years?

**List three goals you'd like to accomplish in the next year.**

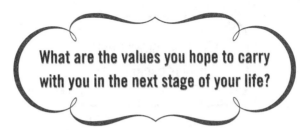

What are the values you hope to carry
with you in the next stage of your life?

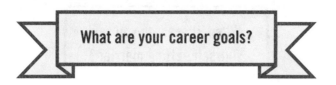

What are your career goals?

When, if ever, do you see yourself getting married?

Do you know who you'll marry?

Write a list of qualities you're looking for in your ideal partner.

## Do you see yourself having kids?

**CIRCLE OR INITIAL YOUR ANSWER.**

YES/NO

**HOW MANY?**

| 1 | 2.4 | 4 |

Gosselin     12     Duggar

**OTHER:**

## What kind of parent will you be?

**CIRCLE OR INITIAL YOUR ANSWER.**

helicopter parent          absent parent

cool parent          drunk parent

dog parent          Real Houseparent

**OTHER:**

Which friend would you choose to plan your bachelorette/conscious uncoupling/singledom celebration party?

## Choose your bridesmaids.
## You can only have four.

1.

2.

3.

4.

Who would be on your
"free pass" list?

Would you ever consider
having an open relationship?

Circle where you'll live in ten years.

**OPTIONS:**

Mansion

Apartment

Shack

House

Ha! That was a MASH reference. Now actually write where you'll live in ten years. Feel free to channel *The Secret*.

Do you have a suspicion
about how you'll die?

**What will your tombstone say?
Write it here.**

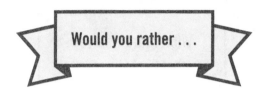

Would you rather . . .

**CIRCLE OR INITIAL YOUR ANSWER.**

a. Die young and hot

b. Join the 27 club

c. Outlive all of your friends

d. Die? What with cryogenesis advances?

**CIRCLE OR INITIAL YOUR ANSWER.**

that 2 a.m. text          sleeping with an ex

not taking that big professional leap

losing touch with friends          not having children

spending too much time at work

not expressing your feelings for someone
until it's too late

**OTHER:**

**What will be your mid-life crisis?**

What retirement home game are you most likely to participate in?

**CIRCLE OR INITIAL YOUR ANSWER.**

a. Bingo

b. Blackjack

c. Mah jongg

d. Strip poker

What would you title your autobiography?
(Subtitles also accepted.)

Describe and/or draw
your friendtopia.

What would your reality show be called?

## What's your future *Real Housewives* tagline?

**FOR EXAMPLE:**

I love gossip, but I don't have any.

Life's too short for me to wait on you.

I'm not too mean, I'm just too honest.

But will there be wine?

What would your *Bachelor* entrance look like?

What are your top future
baby/pet names?

What drink would you name after your friend?
What would be in it?

Draw your wine label.

Draw your future tattoo.

Plan a vacation together.
Where would you go?

What would your traveling
pants item be?

What futuristic technology do you think will become a reality in your lifetime?

Design your own friendship crest.

Plan your dream second wedding
(you know, now that you're rich).

Who's your backup spouse?
If you don't have one,
text your preferred backup now.

# Where is your dream second home?

What job would you want that you've never had the guts to pursue?

**What do you want to do by the time you're thirty?**

**By the time you're forty?**

# Fifty?

How will you celebrate
any future big birthdays?

What will you commit to doing
with your friends every five years?